GOD IS IN THE CRACKS

GOD IS IN THE CRACKS

A NARRATIVE IN VOICES

Robert Sward

Black Moss Press
2006

Copyright © Robert Sward 2006

Library and Archives Canada Cataloguing in Publication

Sward, Robert, 1933-
   God in the cracks / Robert Sward.

Poems.
ISBN 0-88753-422-8

1. Fathers and sons—Poetry, drama. I. Title.

PS8587.W35G63 2006   C811'.54   C2006-902623-8

Author photo by Paul Schraub
Cover design: Karen Veryle Monck

Published by Black Moss Press, 2450 Byng Road, Windsor, Ontario N8W3E8. Black Moss Press acknowledges the generous support of the Canada Council and the Ontario Arts Council for its publishing program.

Le Conseil des Arts | The Canada Council
du Canada | for the Arts

ONTARIO ARTS COUNCIL
CONSEIL DES ARTS DE L'ONTARIO

AUTHOR'S NOTE

As *The Globe and Mail* noted in a review of *The Collected*, from which many of the father poems are reprinted: "The heart and core of this book is a series of dramatic monologues and dialogues between father and son..."

Of Russian-Jewish heritage, my Talmud-conversant father—a Chicago-based podiatrist by profession—came unhinged after my mother, a former Miss Chicago, died at age 42.

In the late '40s he became a Rosicrucian and practised his rites secretly in the basement of our home. Dad evolved his own blend of kabbalistic, Christian hermetic, and prescient New Age mysticism which lent its colors to his medical practice as well as to his view of my eventual career choice and several marriages.

This book draws on *Rosicrucian in the Basement* and *Heavenly Sex* (Black Moss Press) and includes a dozen new poems in the father-son series. The poems here are sequenced to form a narrative spanning 60 years (1945-present) and are best read in the order printed.

ALSO BY ROBERT SWARD

POETRY

Advertisements, Odyssey Chapbook Number One, 1958
Uncle Dog & Other Poems, 1962
Kissing The Dancer & Other Poems, Introduction by William Meredith, 1964
Thousand-Year-Old Fiancée, 1965
Horgbortom Stringbottom, I Am Yours, You Are History, 1970
Hannah's Cartoon, 1970
Quorum/Noah (With Mike Doyle), 1970
Gift, 1971
Five Iowa Poems, 1975
Cheers For Muktananda, 1976
Honey Bear On Lasqueti Island, B.C., 1978
Six Poems, 1980
Twelve Poems, 1982
Movies: Left To Right, 1983
Half-A-Life's History, Poems New & Selected, Introduction by Earle Birney, 1983
The Three Roberts, Premiere Performance, Featuring Robert Priest, Robert Zend and Robert Sward, 1984
The Three Roberts On Love, 1985
The Three Roberts On Childhood, 1985
Poet Santa Cruz, Introduction by Morton Marcus, 1985
Four Incarnations, New & Selected Poems, 1991
Rosicrucian in the Basement, Introduction by William Minor, 2001
Three Dogs and a Parrot, 2001
Heavenly Sex, New & Selected Poems, 2002
The Collected Poems, 1957-2004

FICTION

The Jurassic Shales, A Novel, 1975
Family, with Charles Atkinson, Tilly Shaw, David Swanger, Robert Sward, 1994
A Much-Married Man, A Novel, 1996

NON-FICTION

The Toronto Islands, An Illustrated History, 1983
AUTOBIOGRAPHY, Gale Research / Thomson, *Contemporary Authors*, Volume 206, 2003.

EDITED BY ROBERT SWARD
Vancouver Island Poems, An Anthology, 1973
Emily Carr: The Untold Story, 1978

CDS, DVDS, ELECTRONIC BROADSIDES AND CHAPBOOKS
Rosicrucian in the Basement, as read by the author. (Recorded for the KPFA-FM Program "Cover to Cover," Berkeley, CA), 2002
Robert Sward: Poetry, Review & Interview with Jack Foley (Recorded for the KPFA-FM Program "Cover to Cover," Berkeley, CA), 2002
Writers' Friendship, Jack Foley and Robert Sward (Recorded for the KPFA-FM Program "Cover to Cover," Berkeley, CA), 2003

DVD Muse Magazine, produced and edited by Wallace Boss, Santa Cruz, CA, 2005
wboss@sbcglobal.net

Earthquake Collage, Blue Moon Review, electronic chapbook based on 1989 Loma Prieta earthquake

God is in the Cracks – electronic chapbook, mp3 sound, graphics, seven poems read by the author: http://www.robertsward.com
http://jjwebb.ihwy.com/rosycrossfather/index.html
Video component of the electronic chapbook: http://www.VirtualWorldStudio.com

Grateful acknowledgment is made to the editors of the following publications or media where various of these poems were published, recorded or broadcast:
- Alsop Review
    http://www.alsopreview.com/columns/foley/jfgioiakleinzahler.htm
- Chiron Review
- Faith and Doubt, Anthology, Henry Holt & Co.
- Monterey Bay Poetry Review
- The New Quarterly Anthology (Canada) #95 (special poetry issue)
- Nimrod International Journal #27 (awards issue)
- Passager Poetry Contest / Passager Literary Journal
- Poesy
- Poets & Writers of the Monterey Bay, Anthology
- Poetry Magazine.com
    http://www.poetrymagazine.com/archives/2005/Autmn2005/Current/sward.htm
- *Rosy Cross Father*, an electronic chapbook with mp3 sound, graphics, video by Virtual World Studio, Boulder Creek, CA, and seven poems from *God is in the Cracks* including QuickTime video, *A Man Needs a Place to Stand*, Virtual World Studio and J.J. Webb / Beau Blue Presents
    http://jjwebb.ihwy.com/rosycrossfather/cracks_main2.html
- Writers' Almanac, National Public Radio, *God is in the Cracks* and *Ode to Torpor* read by Garrison Keillor, http://writersalmanac.publicradio.org/programs/2004/03/22/

To Gloria in Excelsis

To my children and grandchildren: Cheryl, Kamala, Michael, Hannah, Nicholas – Aaron, Robin, Maxine, Heron and Per

With thanks to Elissa Alford, Heidi Alford, Jonathan Alford, David Alpaugh, Len Anderson, Charles Atkinson, Ellen Bass, Rose Black, Robert Bly, Wallace Boss, Maria Elena Caballero-Robb, Sondra Cox, Ruth Daigon, Dion Farquhar, Jack Foley, Dana Gioia, Peter Gilford, James D. Houston, Pauline Hymus, Coeleen Kiebert, Allan Lundell and Virtual World Studio, Patrick McCarthy, Morton Marcus, Doug McClellan, Bruce Meyer, William Minor, Robyn Sarah, Tilly Shaw, David Swanger, Hannah Sward, J.J. Webb (Beau Blue Presents) and Joan Zimmerman.

My thanks, as ever, to Marty Gervais and Black Moss Press for years of generosity and commitment to my work.

"For according to the outward man, we are in this world, and according to the inward man, we are in the inward world...

"Since then we are generated out of both worlds, we speak in two languages, and we must be understood also by two languages."
—**Jacob Boehme**

*   *   *

"Who has not experienced the force of passionate love for a woman will never attain to the love of God."
—**Rabbi Eliahu di Vidas**

*   *   *

"Life is full of misery, loneliness, and suffering – and it's all over much too soon."
—**Woody Allen**

*   *   *

"There is a crack, a crack in everything. That's how the light gets in."
—**Leonard Cohen**

CONTENTS

I – GETTING THROUGH THE NIGHT

The Podiatrist's Son 17
    1. Feet is Feet, *Putz* is *Putz* 17
    2. How to Shop for Shoes 19
    3. Getting Through the Night 20
Son of the Commandment 22
What was God Thinking? 24
    1. At the Hospital 24
    2. The End of the World 25
Kaddish 26
    1. Mother's Limousines 26
    2. *Gehenna*, or Purgatory 30
    3. Against Darkness 32
    4. Anniversary 34
The School of Light 36
    1. Science of the Unseen 36
    2. Fraternity of the Earth 37
    3. A Trip to the Zoo 38
Anniversary of Her Death 39

II – WOMEN ARE CRAZY, MEN ARE STUPID

Kit Kat Club 43
Potchkee with the *Pupik* 44
Private Pleasures 45
Sabbath Eve 47
Intimate Geography 48

III – JEW OVERBOARD

Lenore and the Leopard Dog 53
    1. Catahoula Leopard Dog 53
    2. The Mystery of the Mouth 54
    3. The Holiness of Sex 56
    4. Lenore Gets on Top 58
Rosicrucian in the Basement 60
    1. What's to Explain? 60
    2. Jesus 62
    3. Rosy Cross Father 63

Rosicrucian One Dollar Bill 65

IV – MARRIAGE 1, 2, 3, 4

Heavenly Sex 69
    1. The Law 69
    2. The Blessing 69
The Podiatrist Pronounces on His Son's Divorce 70
Wedding #2 71
    1. Temple Parking Lot 71
    2. Temple Steps 72
    3. Temple Washroom 73
Marriage #3 74
Marriage #4 75

V – FEET KNOW THE WAY TO THE OTHER WORLD

One-Stop Foot Shop 79
He Takes Me Back as a Patient 80
God is a Pedestrian 81
Good News from the Other World 84
Arch Supports—The Fitting 86
God is in the Cracks 87
God's Podiatrist 88

VI – DARKNESS IS A CANDLE TOO

After the Bypass 93
    1. In the Hospital 93
    2. Checking Out 94
    3. Course of Study 95
Father, One Week Dead, Strolling Up Palm Canyon Boulevard 97
Dog Door to Heaven 99
Dog, with Father, at their Ease in Heaven 100
A Man Needs a Place to Stand 101
Life is its Own Afterlife 102
From Beyond the Grave, the Podiatrist Counsels His Son on Prayer 103
This is a Father 105

NOTES 106
Kit Kat Club in History 107
The Play "Cabaret" 108
Louisiana Catahoula Leopard Dog 108

I

GETTING THROUGH THE NIGHT

THE PODIATRIST'S SON

When our feet hurt, we hurt all over.
—Socrates

1. *Feet is Feet, Putz is Putz*

Mother:
"The boy has urges.
He's at that age."

Father:
"So?"

"*Shh*. Talk to him, you're a doctor."

"A podiatrist, not a *putzmeister*."

"Please, say something."

"Feet is feet, *putz* is *putz*.
I'll buy him a book."

"Sit already! Breakfast,
sweet rolls, coffee…
Oi, there he is now, sneaking up on us,
Mr. Secrets
      with the half-open eyes, see?
But the mouth, that he keeps shut.
And he scribbles, *oi*!
      scribble, scribble, scribble
he's a *shlimazel*."

"He's a dreamer."

"But unlucky. You know what it means, son,
    shlimazel?
From the German, *shlim*, 'bad' it means,
and *mazel*, this even you know, 'luck.'
   So, *shlimazel*,
   you look into the river,
      the fish drop dead.
   You deal in shrouds,
        people stop dying.
Now you know. Now you know *shlimazel*."

"*Shlimazel?* Unlucky?
Better you think
we shouldn't have a son?
The boy's a dreamer,
he makes things up.
But look, his feet still
aren't on the ground"

"They've never been on the ground.
Dreamer, *schemer*... Listen to me, son,
one day you'll wake up,
    come down to earth
and become a doctor, a real doctor.
Get educated, get married, get out—
Make your mother proud of you."

"He's round-shouldered.
He walks with his head down. See?
And he toes in.

                              Poor feet, poor posture.
                           He's a dreamer. The boy lives
                                 in another world."

"A therapist he should see."

                              "So, we're made of money?"

"Money? Two nurses you have, *shiksas* no less,
x-ray machine, whirlpool, diathermy,
a hospital doesn't have such equipment.
A therapist he should see,
but shoes we can afford."

                                    "That's it, Oxfords,
                                     Florsheims, shoes
                                   that will support him,
                                      shoes with laces,
                                    shoes that breathe."

"Listen, listen to your father."

2. *How To Shop For Shoes*

Seymour Shoes, Maxwell Street, Chicago

                           "No loafers, no sandals, nothing
                                    without laces."

                          "There are fifty-two bones in the feet;
                           thirty-three joints; more than one
                               hundred tendons, muscles and
                                         ligaments…"

> "Fit for length, fit for width,
> get both feet fitted.
>
> "People are asymmetrical. You'll find
> one foot, one testicle, one breast
> larger than the other…"

"Listen, listen to your father."

> "Feet swell, grow larger
> as the day goes on.
>
> "So, *nu?* shop when they're bigger,
> shop for the larger foot.
>
> "Otherwise…
> heel pain, heel spurs, bunions and
> hammertoes…
>
> "Remember, there's no 'break-in period,'
> shoes don't break in.
> Buy what feels right now."

"Born in *shtetl*,
now here he is, a doctor."

3. Getting Through the Night

> "So: the foot is the mirror of health.
> What's that smell?
> Let me see your feet. *Oi!*

"How many times do I have to say it?
A pair of feet have 25,000 sweat glands,
can produce eight ounces, a cup of perspiration in a single day.

"One quarter of all the bones in the
human body are in the feet."

He sits at my bedside carving arch supports.

"Take a flashlight.
Never walk around in the dark.
Most foot fractures occur at night…

"Now remember your slippers," he says
as I head for the bathroom.

In my father's house, there are no bedtime stories.

SON OF THE COMMANDMENT

Chicago

"So, twelve years old! Soon you'll be *bar mitzvah*,
       a *mensch*, a human being. Yes, son,
a human being, you. 'Today I am a man,' you'll say,
like I did. Let's see what you know:
The serpent in the Bible, what language does he speak?

"What's wrong with you? He speaks Hebrew. Same as God.
Same as Abraham and Isaac.
Same as Jesus.
Who else speaks Hebrew?

"Adam and Eve. Noah, too, and the animals:
the giraffe, the kangaroo, the lion.
      Hebrew.
           Hebrew.
Soon you'll speak Hebrew.
Yes, and you'll read it too. *Apostate!*

"You're going to Hebrew School.

"Why? So you can speak to God in His own language.
Lesson One: *Bar* means son, *mitzvah* means commandment.
Bar mitzvah: Son of the commandment.
Commandment, *mitzvah*: What God gave to Moses.

"Lesson Two: When did Jews get souls?

"Souls they got when they got *Torah*.
Torah. *Torah* is Commandments.
Torah is soul.

"So learn, *bar mitzvah* boy! Read. Learn the blessing.
Do it right and you'll see
      the letters fly up to heaven.

"Learn. Yes. There's money
         in puberty,
    money in learning. Books, money, fountain
pens… Always remember: learning is the best merchandise.
"Lesson Three: *Daven* means pray. You rock back and forth
      like the rabbi,
            and pray. In Hebrew.
From your mouth to God's ear.
But it has to be in Hebrew.
And you can't mispronounce:
And no vowels to make it easy."

WHAT WAS GOD THINKING?

1. *At the Hospital*

Father:
"I don't understand. What was God thinking,
    what was He thinking?"

Mother:
"What's to understand?
I'm dead.
We weren't made to last.
What's to understand?
Ach, he doesn't hear me."

"God forgive me.
A good woman. At least may she rest in peace."

"Rest in peace? I'm dead for god sake.
What good will rest do?
You rest in peace.
And something else, my friend, no viewing,
no 'open casket.' They want to look at me, let them
    go look at someone else. Later,
    if they want to visit, fine.
    They know the address.
But no flowers. Tell them. No flowers.
    Flowers die.
Stones they should bring, not flowers.
And as for afterlife, tell them, there is no 'afterlife.'
Look at him. He doesn't hear a word I'm saying."

2. *The End of the World*

"He stripped your mother, son,
      stripped the soul from her body.
You think a human life is not a world?
So then mourn,
      mourn for the end of the world.
And cover the mirrors.
Oi, look at you:
      Take off those shoes.
This is not a time for leather.
Here, let me tear that shirt for you.
Why? Because your mother's dead. God did her in;
her death should cost you something too.
That's right and put ashes on your head.
You're sitting *shiva* now.
      It's the law. You're a Jew.
Read the small print.
Seven days you cannot leave the house.
No radio, no TV, no looking at magazines,
      no books.
You'll see what death is like.
She's gone, so mourn, damn you, mourn!"

KADDISH

May the Great Name be blessed…

1. *Mother's Limousines*

"Mourn like a Jew," Grandfather Max says,
tearing my shirt
          from the collar down,
"and when she's buried, rip out the grass
      and wail.
Expose your heart. Lament for her."

        Mother, mother
        mother of the inflamed heart.

Car door slamming behind us as we exit…

Bar-mitzvah'd boy, 14, I say it once,
say what I'm told to say,
"He is the Rock, His work is perfect…"
Say it,
        YIT-GA-DAL
        V'YIT-KA-DASH
        SH'MEI
        RA-BA
        B'AL MA…
    the Kaddish of sounds, not words

"May a great peace from heaven…" I say,
"May His great Name be blessed,
…Magnified and sanctified…
> *Y'HAY*
> *SH'LAMA*
> *RA-BA*
> *MIN SH'MAYA*
> *V'CHAYIM*
> *ALENU*… I say.

…a week later,
> no to the rabbi,
> no to morning,
> no to twilight,
>> no to the mid-day prayer
no repeating the prayer three times a day for a year
> no, I say, and no to the *shul*.

> "We're animals first and human second,"
> she says, "and there is no God. Do you
> hear me?"

Fox-trotting mother. Dancer mother. Beauty Queen
> in the house of prayer.

> "Mom," I ask, "how do you pray?"
> She shakes her head and turns away.
>> "Snap out of it," she says.

> "Better to go shopping," she says,
> "better to get a job, better to make money."
> I reach out. "Mom—"

"Hands off," she says, "hands off."

"Kids," she says. "*Oi vay.*"
"Holocaust," she says. "*Oi, oi, oi.*"
"God," she says. "What God?"

"Bless the Lord who is blessed," I don't pray.
"May the Great Name be blessed," I don't pray,
    but burn a candle so Mother,
Miss Chicago,
        can find her way back.

    Later, I cannot recall her face.
    "…you're not to look on any photo of her,
        not for seven days," says
           Grandfather.
    What did she even look like?
    Faceless son
        mourning a faceless mother,
        mourning her,
    mourning
        freelance,
    mourning on the fly.

"She'll wander for seven days," Grandfather says,
"then, when she's wormed, her soul will return to God."

    lacks a body and I can't recall her face
    lacks a body and I can't recall her face

"Save her soul from *Gehenna*.
Join us," pleads the rabbi.
           No, no is my prayer
No to duty and no to prayer.

Who was she? Some brunette rich girl
I never knew,
       a stranger dead at 42.
Mother, the beautiful secretary.
I touch her in a dream. She turns,
and there's no one there.

I shake from head to foot.
I stand and I sway.
"Mother, Mother," I say.

Blessed be the stranger.
No, no to the stranger,
no to the stranger.

No is my Kaddish.
No is my prayer.
I am the no
I am the not.

I will not be her savior,
I will not.

2. Gehenna, or Purgatory

        Mother applies Pond's Beauty Cream. Her
        face glistens. Massages her forehead with
        one hand,
        holds the other to her heart.

        "What's the point?" she asks, cigarette
        ablaze,
                mouth tightening.

        When she dies, they bury her not in a
        shroud, but in pancake make-up
        and best gray dress.

"Turn the photos to the wall," says Grandfather,
"and cover your lips.
                      That's right. Now cover your face.
Isolate yourself — groan — let your hair grow wild.
The mourner is the one without a skin, says the Talmud.
Understand? You are no longer whole."
And I think: *I am going to die, too.*

Sit in silence and say nothing.

        "How about a prayer to locusts?" I pray,
        "How about a prayer to boils?

        "O murdering heaven," I pray.

Grandfather cooks lentils,
lentils and eggs. "Mourners' food," he calls it.

"A prayer to rats,
and a prayer to roaches."

"Death is the mother of beauty," he says.
"The death of another makes you want to die," he says.
"The Angel of Death is made entirely of eyes," Grandfather says.

Damn seeing,
Damn touching.
Damn feeling.
Damn loving.

In Jewish hell—

I am the unknowing,
the not Jewish Jew.

Split, cloven,
      cracked

In hell

*name*less,
and eyeless,
          faceless.
No, no to blessings,
no to teachings,
no to reading from right to left.

I pray with them,
I pray with the no, I pray with the not.
I pray with the dead, I pray with the damned.

God, God who is a wound, we pray.

3. Against Darkness

        "Kaddish is a song against darkness," says the rabbi.
        YIT-GA-DAL
        V'YIT-KA-DASH
        SH'MEI
        RA-BA
        B'AL MA…
            "'Magnified and sanctified
            May His Great Name Be…'
        No it says, no to darkness. No to nothingness.
            'May His Great Name be blessed.'
        Kaddish praises God…
        Kaddish: a mourner's prayer
        that never mentions death.
        Y'HAY
        SH'LAMA
        RA-BA
        MIN SH'MAYA
        V'CHAYIM…

"Now then, Let R__, the son of G__,
    come forward," says the rabbi,
but I freeze, pretend not to hear.
Again he calls, calls me to say Kaddish.
(Loudly) "Let R__, son of G__, step beside me."
Ten other mourners turn in my direction.

Again I pretend not to hear.
Staring, face crimson, then white, he turns
    and continues with the service.

The Lord is our God, the Lord is One…
I mourn her — mourn Kaddish — mourn *shul*
and head for home. Age 14, I walk out
      looking
                for stones
I might hurl into heaven.

          *   *   *

    I am the un-*bar'd mitzvah*,
    escaped
        Jew from nowhere,
    apostate,
    skipped Jew,
        cleft Jew,
    Jew, pause in the beating of the heart.

          *   *   *

    Once home, I pray, "Damn Him,
    "damn G-d," I pray.

          *   *   *

Mother, car door slamming,
  the shovel biting
Mother, whose body is the world,
  spinning into space—

"Life rattles," she says.
"My son, His Royal Highness," she says,
  "get used to it."

"Mom, is there an afterlife?"
"Shape up," she says. "You are my afterlife.
  God help us."

4. *Anniversary*

"We're just subdivisions of one person.
One's no better than any other.
Someone dies and you move forward
    into the front lines," Grandfather says,
        lighting a *yortzeit* candle.

    "'Blessed art thou who raises the dead...'"

Shaking the match, he turns. *"Gottenyu!"* he says.
"I should have been next."
Tears well up
    and I see him see her
        in me.

"Same color hair,
    same eyes..." Grandfather says.
"Remember seeing her in her coffin?" he asks,
    grabbing my arm.
"Your mother didn't believe, but she'll be raised
and rest with G-d. Does love quit?

"Can you feel her... hear her inside you?"
I nod.
"Where?"
"Here, in my chest."
"And what does she say?"
"She says nothing," I reply,
    but she does:

"Loopy doop," she says, *"Rest in peace!*
Wait'll you die, you'll see. There is no peace.
When you're dead,
      you're dead.
  Enough.
      Meshugge!" she says, and
      shakes her head.

"Pray, damn you," he says. "It's your mother."

"...Now it's over," he sobs.
 "But you, the un-mourner
will mourn for her all your life.

"Jew, Jew without beginning," he mocks,
"Jew who got away."

THE SCHOOL OF LIGHT

1. Science of the Unseen

"Son, did you know wood decays
at the same rate as the human body?
So what's the good of a casket?
What's the good of a body?
Go, go without sleep!
Goddammit,
it makes you crazy.
Read, then. Read this Rosicrucian.
*The wise man sees in Self those that are alive
and those that are dead.*
Yeats, Yeats,
you should read *The Rose*.
For me now, it's back to school. The inner college.
It's a brotherhood, it's science,
College of the Unseen, but science.
Roses and crosses. *Ach*, you've seen the ad.
Then you've seen the eye of God.
So I wrote away. They sent me this.
Beauty. Splendor.
Mercy. Wisdom.
It's not Jewish, but you think it's not Jewish?
It's not so not Jewish.
Nightmares. Your dead mother. *Oi.*
A man needs to get through the night."

2. *Fraternity of the Earth*

"'Beyond the point where nothing is known
      is called The Beginning.
Within The Beginning, the Unknown created God.'
Talmud says. And this they teach,
      the Rosicrucians.
Over here, son, can you smell?
Roses, roses and incense…
the aroma of infinity.
Ach, what would you know?
You, you think it's easy?
Burlap bags she patched,
      so we could eat.
And could she read, your grandmother?
In *shtetl*, in Poltava, who could read?
But look, *The Chicago Tribune, Popular Mechanics*…
Here, an ad again, the School of Light, see?
'Holiness pervades physical matter.'
And you, questions, questions…
'What is Rosicrucian? What is Rosicrucian?'
A fraternity, a brotherhood…
Enough. She's dead, your mother, I need this.
A man needs to get through the night."

3. A Trip to the Zoo

"Lead into gold, easy!
But I need a fraternity,
      that's right, a fraternity.
            Brotherhood,
                the Fraternity of the Earth.
Why? To learn the language, do the alchemy.
Here, I'm going to pull an eyelash.
Now, under a microscope...
              mites, bacteria, fungi, see?
I'm your father, but what am I? A zoo.
You're my son, but what are you? Also, a zoo.
Yes, there's a universe in a grain of sand,
a father—10,000 fathers—
      and sons too
           in this one eyelash.
So, as many creatures on our bodies
as there are universes, as there are fathers, as there are zoos,
      zoos, zoos, and the zoos of zoos.
You think you're alone?
Here, son, a Rosicrucian eyelash."

ANNIVERSARY OF HER DEATH

At the Rosicrucian Altar

Sweeps away incense and candles,
      liquid-filled crystal flask…
"Forget prayer, forget everything I ever said."
Bolts the door, pours himself a drink.

          Said about what, dad?

"What? Prayer. *Everything*. Forget it!
God doesn't need your prayer.
Now put on your shoes and get out of here."

          **But dad, this stuff is just beginning
          to make sense.**

"Nonsense," he says.

          What about the unseen?

"Goddammit, if it isn't seen,
      it isn't there.
She's dead. Your mother's dead.
What are you, stupid?"
Reaches for matches. Lights a cigarette.

          But what about… soul?

"Soul? You know better than that.
There is no soul."

And 'the other side'?

"There is no other side. You want to know
what's on the other side? Nothing.
That's what's on the other side.
Ach, you're looking for meaning.
      Meaning's on backorder.
The sun and the moon and the stars,
      they're all on backorder.
Nothing's there. Nothing ever existed.
      She's dead. Don't you get it? The world is just a word.
Talmud says.
      Earth is a flaming word.
That's it. That's it. End of story."

II

WOMEN ARE CRAZY, MEN ARE STUPID

KIT KAT CLUB
Chicago, 1948

"That one, the blonde, if she asks you, buy her a drink!
Here's your Scotch. We're here to enjoy.
Be happy! Enough mourning.
You're fifteen. At thirteen even
a boy becomes a man. Goddammit,
it's not every son gets to drink with his father.
So stand straight. Think! Two men alone,
      a year now
she's dead. What are we? Rabbi says, 'A pinch of air
in a wooden box.' You. Me. Your mother.
Tonight you're gonna see,
      you're here to learn. You know what it is, life?
A terminal condition.
There she is now, dancing, Miss Gina Lynn.
Goddammit, for your own good I brought you.
So stop fidgeting. Here, have a cigarette.
And Miss Delecta d'Lotta, the blonde.
Oi, such a *tuchis*!
Look at her now, she's got her whozis on the table,
      the men line up, *oi!*
and for what do you think? Show's beginning! For a kiss,
      that's right.
Twenty dollars to put your tongue God knows where!
What? Goddammit, what do you think they're doing?
They're doing what they're doing.
Bartender, fill 'em up!
Oi, what fathers won't do for their sons!"

POTCHKEE WITH THE *PUPIK*

"So now you know.
        This is America. This is what people do.
In Poltava, in *shtetl*, you think they *potchkee*
        with the *pupik*?
Now what? Listen! She's asking for something. A light?
Ach, look at that! A cigarette d'Lotta's smoking.
And now what? Now, *now* what's smoking?
Feh! Who told you to look?
Women are crazy, men are stupid.

"We're here tonight so you can see, *farshtehst*?
With your own eyes now what do you see?
        A beautiful woman.
Oi, high heels she wears, painted toenails—pink!
        ankle chain, and such a smile,
and look, look at those eyes…
        Ach, my eyes water.

"She's finished. Talk to her, go, go now
before she puts on her clothes.
'Young lady, Miss d'Lotta,' say,
'the doctor wants to buy you a drink,' tell her
        quick, quick,
before she leaves…"

PRIVATE PLEASURES

Delecta d'Lotta leans over the table.

"So, what is it, gentlemen, a private booth?
A bottle of champagne?

"Just remember, no touching…
unless I say so. Hands
      at your side, tongue in your mouth.

"What I do on stage, I do on stage.
Off stage we give it a rest.
Here, talk is what we do.
      —Yeah, that's right, I'm a big girl…
         like my friend Gypsy.

"What's that, Sonny? You want to touch?
Hey, Randy,
    a magnum of champagne!
        Fifty bucks, fellas…
Pop, your son says you're a doctor.

—"Oh, really, a po-di-atrist? Well, fella, I'm an ec-dy-si-ast.
—An ecdysiast? A stripper…
Ec-dy-sis, it's a snake word, it means to shed
    your skin. Fuckin' snakes, I hate 'em!

"C'mon, kid, I got somethin' for you. Here, gimme your hand,
    it's okay, huh?
You like that? Now pay attention.
    There's a person
        right behind
    what you see. That's it, a person
        inside a person.

"Sound familiar, doc? Enough already, admit it,
      your kid knows, don't you, Sonny?
Your old man's here all the time.
'We're naked in heaven, but clothed on earth,'
      whatever that means.
'A dancer in two worlds.' Sure, sure.

"You know, some guys, it's like they're blind.
They won't look, just being in a room with naked girls,
I guess, that's enough.

"Others get hooked on a certain girl,
      a pole dancer, say, and their eyes roll up.

"Do men have souls? Some, some I know—
      they'd trade, that's right,
         soul for pussy.
Your dad says 'loneliness is the maker of the soul.'
'Bullshit,' I say, 'no soul without pussy. Men will do anything to get it,
      not once they've got it, but to get it.
So the power of pussy is golden. But once they got it, forget it.'

"Randy, cognacs all around—goes good with champagne!
Hey, boys you know this song?

"'...*Yes, I'm the money girl,*
      the honey girl.
Down is up
      and up is down
and darkness is my candle.'

"You like that, fellas?
Well, look at this, look at this...
That's right. Now we're getting somewhere, okay?"

SABBATH EVE

"*Oi*, now where'd she go?
Listen, quick! she'll be right back.
I'll leave… and then what?
You need to know *Shekinah*,
        —*Shekinah?*
God's 'dwelling place' it means. Rabbi says.
He needs it. The Lord needs her.
God has no home without her.

"Star of David tells the story.
Man on the bottom, woman on the top,
this is what it means:
Quick, quick, she's coming…

"The upward triangle
    of the Star of David
is a penis
    penetrating the downward triangle of the vulva.
Shekinah, God's 'dwelling place,'
    Talmud says.
It means: no female, no soul.
So, when the *schtupping* stops,
the world ends."

INTIMATE GEOGRAPHY

"Look at her, singing again!"

"*'Tall men, short men,*
  fat men, thin,
they kiss with theirs
  and I kiss with mine.

  Down is up
 and up is down
and darkness is my candle.'

      *   *   *

"Drink up! Time to order another.
Scotch, Randy, Scotch all around.

—"'*The female soul of God…*'?
What's he talking about now?
This is a spread club, a *spread* club,—
and he comes here and talks about 'soul'?

"You're not the first, doc, or am I just lucky?
Brainy guys, they don't know if they want a lap dance
or a head massage.
The '*female soul of God!*' I'll show you
  the female soul of God.
"You know what Gypsy said, don't you? 'God is love,
  but get it in writing.'
A dollar bill, now that gets it in writing.

"Alright, suppose God has what you say, a female soul,
  then She feels something, like Gypsy and me.
God has feelings too.

—"What, yeah, I'm a convent girl,
Our Lady of the Vagina.
And my little dance, my *'shtick'*?
Look, if you don't have a gimmick
      you're not going to be a star.

"So, doc, you want a word
      with the female soul?
           The 'front door to life'?
Okay, guys, I'll show you.
Pull up a chair.

"But doc, maybe you should leave.
I'll look after the kid.
      He's legal isn't he?
How 'bout another Scotch, kid?
Wanna sing with me? You know the words?

'One, two three
      You're lookin' good to me…'

"What do you say, Sonny, wanna take the wheel,
      give it a whirl?"

'Four, five, six…'"

"Last chance… yep, here we go, baby… that's it…

'I wanna kiss your lips.'

"Come to Momma, come to Momma…"

III

JEW OVERBOARD

LENORE AND THE LEOPARD DOG

Father's heart attacks him.

1. Catahoula Leopard Dog

Lenore K. appears at our door.
Father greets her. He wears
      a silk bathrobe,
big horn-rimmed glasses
and his eyes bob up and down;
"I'm feeling better…"

        You better be better.

Lenore shakes out her shoulder-length,
      silvery-blond hair.
Poppa's eyes widen. Heart attack or no heart attack,
he's ready. Already he's ready.

LOOK, ALREADY HE'S READY, says Leopard Dog,
racing room to room, one brown eye,
one blue eye, sizing me up.
LIKE IT OR NOT, SONNY, WE'RE HERE TO STAY.

      Oh, why, hello there, Sonny.
      I'm Daddy's new friend.

      And that, that meshugge
      is a Catahoula Leopard Dog… see the spots?
      And smart. He understands everything.

"A handsome wife develops the mind of man," Father says.

"No, please, dad," I whisper, "I don't want her,
I don't want another mother."

                          He cups my face
        in his hand.
"Goddammit, I've told you, it's not good
for a man to be alone. And you need a mother."

Leopard dog wags his tail. *WOOF, WOOF*. Stands
on his hind legs, paws on my shoulders.
WE'RE MOVING IN, *FARSHTEHST*?
Springs across the room, switches on
    I Love Lucy.

Lenore sets the table.

                What a dog! He just loves television. Mmm…
                that Ricky Ricardo, look at those yummy
                bedroom eyes.

Shh, says Father.

                You told me yourself, God is right there
                in the pleasure. O, you're good, doctor,
                you're good, she whispers.

2. The Mystery of the Mouth

Later that night

"Your breasts are like twins, young roes
which feed
        among the lilies."

54

Leopard Dog and I listen at the door.

What are you talking about, honey?

AH, HERE COME THE BIRDS AND BEES, says Dog.

"It's in the Bible. A woman's breasts
are the Ten Commandments, the two tablets
of God's law. One for what God allows,
       one for what He doesn't."

Talk sense. You're a doctor, she laughs.

I peek through the keyhole.

Father's kneeling by the bed, pouring wine.

What about kissing?

"Kissing is praying too, darling. Look, I bow my head,
same as when I pray."

"They make me sick," I say.

"I've told you before, dear, God rewards you for kissing."

Lenore sits up in bed. *Whaa—?*

"The way we make love is the way God will be with us.
With the mouth alone it is possible. That's right, darling,
that's the mystery of the mouth."

Leopard dog wags his tail.
THIS IS GOOD, he says.

"Shut up. You're a stupid dog," I say. "What do you know?"

I KNOW YES AND NO
AND *BOW WOW*. GOOD DOG,
BAD DOG. I KNOW PLAY
AND STAY. LICK I KNOW
AND SNIFF I KNOW. *BOW WOW*,
BOW WOW, WHAT DO YOU KNOW?

"Who's that?" Father yells.

> *That's just Leopard. He knows we're in here.*
> *He's lonely. Darling, would you mind?*
> *He likes to watch.*

"What?"

> *You know what I'm saying. He's just a dog.*

3. The Holiness in Sex

G<small>R-R-R</small>— Leopard on his haunches
peeping through the keyhole.

"Hey, move over, Dog, scram!"

Leopard Dog snaps at my hand,
        eyes like cracked glass.

LOOK OUT. I EAT LITTLE BOYS FOR BREAKFAST!

"The socks come off and the feet talk," Father says.

Your father's all muscle.
Who would have thought?
Lenore likes that. They're a match.
That's your new mother.

"The way to heaven is not up, but down.
Love—marriage—intercourse, what are they, darling?
A tangling of toes, right?
        So, how does this feel, Lenore?
Good… and this?"

        Oh, doctor, doctor… You know,
        I like professional men… full of surprises.
        Crazy talk. Silly exams… touching…
        and nice pajamas.

There they go, sonny.

"The holiness derives from feeling the pleasure," Father says.
"No pleasure, no holiness."

Ooo, wicky, wicky, says Leopard Dog,
that's how you were made, little boy.
No wicky wicky, no little boy.

"Move, darling, move, you need to move!"

Look at that. It's heels over bedposts.
It's wicky wicky he loves, not you, sonny.

4. Lenore Gets on Top

Father sits on the side of the bed
        whinnying like a horse.
That lady does it too.

"So look at us," he says,
        reaching for her.
"we're invisible, that's what we are."

        Invisible?

"Invisible, yes: no boundary between exterior and interior.
Tell me, darling, where do I leave off and you begin?
Inside you is inside me. Outside you is outside me.
We're both the same.
So, *nu*, who sees that? Who sees us? We're invisible."

        Luftmensch, head in the clouds.
        You miss this, doctor, and you miss that.
        You think that makes you a mystic?
        Invisible? I'll show you invisible.

WHAT, YOU STILL DON'T GET IT? says Dog,
        thwacking me with his tail.
LENORE'S YOUR MOMMY, LITTLE BOY;
WICKY WICKY'S YOUR FATHER.
YOU HAD A MOTHER.
NOW YOU HAVE ANOTHER.

Hands on his shoulders, she sits on father,
moves up and down.

Now you see it, now you don't, she says.

Bad lenore, bad. That's not dog, says Dog,
    barking at the keyhole.

"There is man and woman and a third thing, too,
in us, says the poet. That's the eye in the heart
that sees into the invisible. The goal, Poet says, is to see
with the eye of the heart so like sees like."

Shut up, she says, *shut up and schtupp.*

"Oh God, marry me," he says, "marry me."

ROSICRUCIAN IN THE BASEMENT

i.
"What's to explain?" he asks.
He's a closet meditator. Rosicrucian in the basement.
In my father's eyes: dream.
"There are two worlds," he says,
liquid-filled crystal flask
                and yellow glass egg
on the altar.
He's the "professional man"—
      so she calls him, my stepmother.
That, and "the Doctor":
"The Doctor will see you now," she says,
      working as his receptionist.
He's a podiatrist—foot surgery a specialty—
      on Chicago's North Side.
Russian-born Orthodox Jew
      with *zaftig* Polish wife, posh silvery white starlet
      Hilton Hotel hostess.

ii.
This is his secret.
This is where he goes when he's not making money.
The way to the other world is into the basement
and he can't live without this other world.
"If he has to, he has to," my stepmother shrugs.
Keeps door locked when he's not down there.
Keeps the door locked when he is.
"Two nuts in the mini-bar," she mutters, banging pots
      in the kitchen upstairs.
Anyway, she needs to protect the family.
"Jew overboard," she yells, banging dishes.
"Peasant!" he yells back.

iii.
"There are two worlds," he says lighting incense, "the seen
and the unseen, and she doesn't understand.
This is my treasure," he says,
            lead cooking in an iron pan,
liquid darkness and some gold.
"Son, there are three souls: one, the Supernal;
      two, the concealed
                       female soul, soul like glue…
holds it all together…"
"And the third?" I ask.
We stand there. "I can't recall."
He begins to chant and wave incense.
No *tallis*, no *yarmulke*,
just knotty pine walls and mini-bar
      size of a ouija board,
a little schnapps and shot glasses
on the lower shelf,
and I'm no help.
Just back from seven thousand dollar trip,
four weeks with Swami Muktananda,
                       thinking
Now there's someone who knew how to convert
the soul's longing into gold.
Father, my father: he has this emerald tablet
      with a single word written on it
and an arrow pointing.

2.
JESUS

"What's with the cross? You believe in Jesus, dad?"
"What?"
"Are you still a Jew?"
He turns away.
"Dammit, it's not a religion, *farshtehst*?"
    Brings fist down on the altar.
"We seek the perfection of metals," he says,
    re-lighting stove,
        "salvation by smelting."

"But what's the point?" I ask.

"The point? Internal alchemy, *shmegegge*. *Rosa mystica*," he shouts.
"Meat into spirit, darkness into light."

Seated now, seated on bar stools.
Flickering candle in a windowless room.
Visible and invisible. Face of my father
    in the other world.
I see him, see him in me
my rosy cross
        podiatrist father.
"I'm making no secret of this secret," he says,
turning to the altar.
"Tell me, tell me how to pray."
"Burst," he says, "burst like a star."

3.
ROSY CROSS FATHER

"Yes, he still believes. Imagine—
    American Jews,
        when they die,
roll underground for three days
to reach the Holy Land.
He believes that."

We're standing at the Rosicrucian mini-bar listening,
(clash of pots in the kitchen upstairs)
        father
    with thick, dark-rimmed glasses
blue-denim shirt,
    bristly white mustache,
    dome forehead.

"Your stepmother's on the phone with her sister," he says.

"He thinks he can look into the invisible,"
    she says from above.
"He thinks he can peek into the other world,
like God's out there waiting for him…
Meshugge!"

She starts the dishwasher.

"As above, so below," he says.
"I'm not so sure," I say.
"Listen, everyone's got some stink," he says,
    grabbing my arm,
        "you think you're immune?"
I shake my head.

"To look for God is to find Him," he says.
"If God lived on earth," she says, "people would knock out
 all His windows."
"*Kibbitzer,*" he yells back. "*Gottenyu! Shiksa brain!*"

Father turns to his "apparatus,"
"visual scriptures," he calls them,
 tinctures and elixirs,
 the silvery dark and the silvery white.

"We of the here-and-now, pay our respects
to the invisible.
 Your soul is a soul," he says, turning to me,
"but body is a soul, too. As the poet says,
'we are the bees of the golden hive of the invisible.'"
"What poet, Dad?"
"The poet! Goddammit, the poet," he yells.

He's paler these days, showing more forehead,
 thinning down.

"We live in darkness and it looks like light.
Now listen to me: I'm unhooking from the world, understand?
Everything is a covering,
contains its opposite.
The demonic is rooted in the divine.
Son, you're an Outside," he says,
 "waiting for an Inside.
but I want you to know…"
"Know what, Dad?"
"I'm gonna keep a place for you in the other world."

ROSICRUCIAN ONE DOLLAR BILL

"Franklin was a Rosicrucian.
He made it. He made
     the one dollar bill.
Open your wallet, take out a dollar.
Money talks, in pictures
     it talks. See,
          Egyptian pyramid.
Money, American money
     with a pyramid.
The eagle, that you understand,
     thunderbolts in one hand,
olive branch in the other.
So, the pyramid,
     what does *that* say?
'You have no idea,' it says,
'you don't know the value of money.
Money is to remind you
what's important in life.' Look:
see, a halo with lines…
     above the pyramid,
'Glory,' that's what they call it,
a 'Glory,' burst of light
with the eye of God inside.
But the pyramid is unfinished, it needs work, like you.

"'*Ach*, enough! Enough with money,' says money.
Just remember, God has His eye on you.
And the sun and the moon and the stars are inside you.
So listen, listen to the pyramid.
You can't buy your way into heaven, it's true,
but you need to know money to get there."

IV

MARRIAGE 1, 2, 3, 4

HEAVENLY SEX

1. The Law

Opens a bottle of schnapps. "Writer, *schmyter*,
you're unemployed.
Unemployed people must make love
at least once a day.
Talmud says:
      A laborer, twice a week; a mule driver
once a week; a camel driver,
once a month. It's the law.
      This is heavenly sex. Say a blessing—
pray— 'Blessed art thou, O Lord our God…'
Ba-ruch a-ta…
For your spouse and for your seed.
What is it with you?
I need to explain how to bring a soul into the world?"

2. The Blessing

"Listen:
The soul is the Lord's candle.
So you say a blessing. And you sing to her—your wife:
Strength and honor are her clothing, you sing.
She openeth her mouth with wisdom, you sing.
Her children arise up and call her blessed, you sing.
Rabbi says if knowing a woman were not holy,
      it would not be called 'knowing.'
So, after a good *Shabbes* meal—
      linen tablecloth, blessed spices,
braided loaves of *challah*,
           a goblet of wine…
Thirty-nine things you cannot do on the Sabbath,
but you can eat. You can drink. You can *schtupp*.
Make one another happy.
It's the law."

THE PODIATRIST PRONOUNCES ON HIS SON'S DIVORCE

"The time for sorry is past.
When a Jew gets divorced, even the altar sheds tears.
    Rabbi says.
Look at these X-rays, perfect daughter.
Her feet we can fix. This is not a problem.
    Perfect little girl,
    just a little knock-kneed.
My God, this is your daughter, a daughter
you're leaving! Five thousand steps a day women take.
Fifty thousand miles in a lifetime. Where will that take her?
    And where will you be?
Other people He created from the feet up
    and at the end they get a brain.
But you it's the other way around—and He forgot the feet.
All these years, all these years, and you got nothing on the ground.
In this life there are two things, son:
Children and money,
    and in that order. What else?
Ach, so leave, leave if leaving is what you're going to do.
You're not going anywhere.
Truth is, you're not going anywhere anyway."

WEDDING #2

1. Temple Parking Lot

Father, removing glasses:
"So, my son is getting married!"

For the second time, dad.

"Yes, but weddings heal. Our Talmud says
 a wedding frees bride and groom
  from all past transgressions.
A wedding fixes all that's broken."

You mean one marriage can fix another?

He grabs my arm: "A happy marriage
gives eternal dispensation."

His eyes gather light.
"The Talmud says intercourse is one-sixtieth
the pleasure of paradise."

I'm wearing five-eyelet Florsheims
 with new arch supports.

"This is good." He waves to friends.
"Just don't fumble the goblet."

The goblet?

"The goblet you break after the vows.
This time use your heel. Smash it on the first try.
People'll be watching. Miss it and they'll laugh—
    like last time.
Don't fumble the goblet."

2. Temple Steps

Leads with his chin.
Visible and invisible.
Chin trembling, his face shining.

"I was an orphan."

    Yes, I know, dad.

"Did you know an orphan's dead parents
    are able to attend the wedding?"

    But dad, I'm not an orphan.

"Well, I just want you to know if you were,
    we'd come anyway.
You know, your grandparents will be there too."

    How will they manage that?

"What are you asking? They'll manage.
These are your grandparents:
Grandpa Hyman. Grandmother Bessie.

It's a tradition. Our Talmud says
if they have their bodies, they'll come with their bodies."
But they're dead.

"So, they'll come without."

3. Temple Washroom

"When a man unites with his wife,
God is between them.
I'm telling you: lovemaking is ceremony.
The Talmud says.
You, you're not holy, but your wife is.
With her
      you go to a world outside the world."

So?

"So wash your hands before
      not after.
Wash for the pure and holy bride."

But what about hygiene?

"How did I bring you up?
Shame on you.
The socks come off and you make love.
The Talmud says. And you make her happy.
Schtupp. Schtupp. Do you understand?
Forget hygiene!
This is the pure and holy bride."

MARRIAGE #3

"Again? That's it.
This time marriage divorces you.
Just walk, walk now, keep walking.
Dr. Neusome's son eats and becomes sensible.
Horse radish, bagels, lox, cream cheese—
A *mensch*. Honorable.
But you, horseradish turns into what?
Divorce.
Bagels into divorce. Cream cheese
into divorce.
You know *schlemiel*? A *schlemiel* trips
      and knocks down the *schlimazel*.
So which are you?
A love weasel, that's what you are.
He obtains a blessing, beautiful
      young woman,
and out it comes, divorce.
With each divorce the *mensch* in you
      gets split in two.
And there's no money in it.
Divide down the middle,
      right down the middle,
Half of a half of a half…
The middle? This time
      there is no middle.
And now the yoga…
The podiatrist's son walks now on his head.
Another blessing. Head over heels didn't work. So, *nu*,
now it's heels over head.
Yes, feet in the clouds, *ach*.
Such a blessing!
Fine, fine! Stand on your head if you like.
Some part of you at least will touch the ground."

MARRIAGE #4

Palm Springs, CA

"One, two, three… Shame
And more children than you can count.
Meshugge.
What have you learned? And now a fourth.
Everything in the world has meaning.
    So, *nu*, tell me:
What's the meaning of this?
Earth, air, fire and foolishness…
The sun and the moon and the stars.
These I understand.
Hieroglyphics I understand.
But you! How many times does a foot marry a foot?
A man should tangle feet with one woman.
One pair of feet. One family. One home.
How many do you need?
    'How's your son?' Mrs. Goldberg asks me.
    'Fine, fine,' I say. 'He's getting married.'
    'Ah, mazel tov, doctor!'
    Three years later she says,
    'So, how's the boy?'
    'Fine, fine. He's married again.'
    'Oi vay!' she says, 'children…'
    She's been through it too.
People say it's human to want to put an end to things.
Well, not for those with their feet on the ground.
Look at your clever face in the mirror: Look,
    look at yourself. Now count:
one face, one face you see, not four.
So, better that part of you with brains
should take off its socks and study feet. For that…
you don't need a mirror."

V

FEET KNOW THE WAY TO THE OTHER WORLD

ONE-STOP FOOT SHOP

               "We walk with angels
and they are our feet.

"'Vibrating energy packets,'" he calls them. "'Bundles of soul
in a world of meat.' Early warning system—
               dry skin and brittle nails;
feelings of numbness and cold;
these are symptoms; they mean something.
I see things physicians miss.

"All you have to do is open your eyes, just open your eyes,
and you'll see: seven-eighths of everything is invisible, a spirit
inside the spirit.
The soul is rooted in the foot.
As your friend Bly says, 'The soul longs to go down';
feet know the way to the other world,
that world where people are awake.
So do me a favor: dream me no dreams.
A dreamer is someone who's asleep.

"You know, the material world is infinite,
but boring infinite," he says, cigarette in hand,
little wings fluttering at his ankles.

"And women," he says, smacking his head,
"four times as many foot problems as men.
High heels are the culprit.

"I may be a podiatrist, but I know what I'm about:
feet. Feet don't lie,
       don't cheat, don't kiss ass. Truth is,
peoples' feet are too good for them."

HE TAKES ME BACK AS A PATIENT

"So there they are, on a pedestal
    your feet under lights.
More than you deserve,
you and those prima donnas.
Villains!" He points a finger.
"With normal people the socks come off
    and the feet talk. But not these two.
Wise guys. Too good for diagnosis, huh?
Too good for arch supports? Is that it?
Your X-ray shows nothing. Ultra sound
    nothing.
This is your last chance. This is it.
Weak ankles, feet out of alignment,
    but there's something else.
I see it in your posture. You're holding back,
    you and those feet of yours,
        slippery feet,
meshugge feet,
    feet like no one else in the family.
What's going on in there?" he asks.
"Wake up! Tell you what:
we're gonna have you walk around the office.
That's it. Head erect,
    back straight.
No, no! Look at you, look at you: you call that walking?
On the ground, on the ground!
Dreamer! *Ach!* You're fired! Your mother was right.
You and those feet of yours are two of a kind."

GOD IS A PEDESTRIAN

Palm Springs, CA

"Trust water, son, you can't go wrong with water.
See, and it's got dual arm rests,
multi-directional
       massage jets,
pneumatic air switch,
a four-horsepower motor

"So, hold here, hold the grab bar—
get in, son. Take a ride on the plumbing express!

"Good for the feet,
good for the back.
Foot problems,
back problems,
       they go together!"

I'm swept away.

"*Schlimazel!* Hydrotherapy is your friend. Hold the grab bar,"
       he yells.

"You want to know a secret?"

Please, dad, no philosophy.

"God is a pedestrian. God who is in heaven
       is also a man, just like you and me."

And what about angels?

"I'm telling you, if they looked after their feet
      they wouldn't need to fly."

Dad, you're nuts.

"Of course, everything is imagination. Rosicrucian says."

Rosicrucian?

"One saw the world in a grain of sand.
So, *nu?* I see it in a pair of feet."

No, dad, not feet again.

"Yes, feet. Feet. The sun and the moon and the stars.
Feet, feet are heaven, too, a heaven filled with stars.
Rosicrucian says. The world is a man and the light of the sun
and the stars is his body."

This is Rosicrucian?

"*Goyisheh kop!* Think! The two are one:
God exists in man so body is a form of soul.
Heal the soul and you heal the body.
Heal the foot and you heal the soul.
That world is in this world, and this world is in that."

So what are you saying, dad?
Maybe there is no 'other side.'

"What am I saying? Wake up!
This is the other side. You're there," he says,
handing me a towel, "right
here, right now. You're home."

GOOD NEWS FROM THE OTHER WORLD

Palm Springs, CA

"Dad, you're lookin' good," I say,
"like the fountain of youth."

His hands on my feet, grimacing, weary,
mercurial, wing-footed
eighty-year-old doctor.

Wears a denim shirt, bola tie,
turquoise and silver tip,
tanned, tennis-playing, macho…

"Making more money now,
more than in Skokie.
But you need arch supports," he says,
encasing my feet in plaster.

Damaged feet. Feet out of alignment.
Four-times married, forty-year-old feet.

"Well, good news from the other world," he says.

"Really?"

"The void is nothing but people's breath."

"So something survives?" I say,

"Feet survive. Feet and breath survive," he says,
"peoples' feet and peoples' breath."

"That *is* good news," I say.

"Don't mock me," he says.
"Do you know you still 'toe in'?
 That your head 'pitches forward'?
You're past the half-way mark, son.
God is not altruistic, you know,
He doesn't make exceptions.
Of course things are dark and light at once."

Huh? Who *is* he? Whoever was my father?

Bloodied in some Russian pogrom.
Nixon-lover on the North Side of Chicago.
Blue denim, bola tie Republican.

Rosicrucian cowboy in the Promised Land.

ARCH SUPPORTS—THE FITTING

Greets me in the waiting room,
father with waxed,
      five-eyelet shoes;
son, too, with spit-shine, five-eyelet shoes.
This is how I was brought up. I do it
      to show respect.
Value your feet.

"Okay, un-sock those feet of yours," he says,
"let's see the felons."
I unlace my Florsheims: moist feet emerging
from their cave of leather.
Father holds up arch supports.
Curved knife in hand, he shakes his head
      as he trims *just so*.

"Remind me. Why do I need these things?" I ask.
"Weak ankles and spine," he says. "Poor posture.
Your feet are fine.
Truth is, you should be more like your feet.
Robust, healthy feet.
Take a lesson from your feet," he says.
"Feet appreciate
      custom made.
No Dr. Scholl's for these feet."

Slips in the inserts.
Arch support like a shoe
inside a shoe,
leather inside leather.

"Every step I take you're going to be there," I say.
"Every step," he says, "every step of the way."

GOD IS IN THE CRACKS

"Just a tiny crack separates this world
from the next, and you step over it
      every day,
God is in the cracks."
Foot propped up, nurse hovering, phone ringing.
"Relax and breathe from your heels.
Now, that's breathing.
So, tell me, have you enrolled yet?"

"Enrolled?"

"In the Illinois College of Podiatry."

"Dad, I have a job. I teach."

"Ha! Well, I'm a man of the lower extremities."

"Dad, I'm forty-three."

"So what? I'm eighty. I knew you
before you began wearing shoes.
Too good for feet?" he asks.
"I. Me. Mind:
              That's all I get from your poetry.
Your words lack feet. Forget the mind.
Mind is all over the place. There's no support.
You want me to be proud of you? Be a foot man.
Here, son," he says, handing me back my shoes,
"try walking in these.
Arch supports. Now there's a subject.
Some day you'll write about arch supports."

GOD'S PODIATRIST

Palm Springs, CA

Corns, calluses, pain
      in the joints of my toes.
Masked man in the half light,
starched white jacket and pants,
      shaking his head.
"Dad, what are you doing?"
"Re-fitting the supports.
What is it with you?" he asks,
"Why don't you respond?
I've never seen such feet.
With a word, the world came into being," he murmurs,
cigarette in hand.
"With you, with arch supports even
      there are these feet that go nowhere.
Anyway, there's just one person,
God, God's body," he says.
"God has a body?" I ask.
"Of course he has a body, and feet.
"Feet?"
"*Feet*, of course feet.
You know he's not one to ask for help."
      Throws me my shoes. "You're finished."
"Help?" I ask.
"It's the least I can do," he says.
"You're a podiatrist for God?" I ask.
"Varicose veins.
The aroma of infinity.

feet sparking, feet an endless ocean,
                        feet made of music.
Of course I have to sort out foot from hallucination.
You can't treat a halo.
Don't look at me like that.
You're the one who doesn't respond to treatment.
God has feet like anyone else. You know it and I know it."
"I am that I am," I say.
"Says you," says my father.
"He is that he is and I'm his podiatrist.
What a son," he says.

VI

DARKNESS IS A CANDLE TOO

AFTER THE BYPASS

Palm Springs, CA

1. *In The Hospital*

"Don't trust the world, son. It's filled
with holes. The best thing is to love…"

     Love what, dad?

"Emptiness. I've been meaning to tell you:
There's a giant scroll suspended below the world
   and it says this world
      is made from letters and numbers
and every number is infinite.
Anyway, I'm invisible, son."

    Dad, I can see you.

"You have two fathers,
     one you can see,
one who looks like me;
  and one you can't,
the father you'll never see.
The invisible *is* invisible,
but I need to make a living.
I'm a doctor, *nu?* What good is a doctor
if you can't see him?
Don't look at me like that. I'm still a Jew,
but some days all I see is Roses and Crosses.
Did you know the male body has nine holes in it?
Seven of those holes are in the head. So there you have it.
The world is a leaky boat, son."

2. *Checking Out*

Rosy cheeked father in a wheel chair.
He pulls out a toothpick. Makes little sucking noises
with his teeth. "Hospital food. Not as bad as they say."

Lights a cigarette.

"She's against it."

Who?

"Who do you think? She's against
the invisible."

Throws away the toothpick.

"I've fallen into a place where everything is music.
You know, if people could take a pill
and become invisible
there would be nobody in sight. It's true. The world
     is made of love,
of our love for emptiness.
Ach, what the hell! Visible, invisible,
     It's all the same.
Still, the world you go round thinking you can see
is filled with holes, and for every hole
     in this world
     there's a hole in the other. If you look,
you can see through the cracks.
I have a treasure now, it's true,
     but no body.
And you, you *meshugge*, you have a body,
but no treasure.
You should take the year off. Spend some time
at the Invisible College."

3. *Course of Study*

Lesson #1

"Stars ejaculate. That's how the world
    came into being.
From sperm. The Sperm of the Stars."

Lesson #2

"There is no place empty of God.

"Darkness is a candle, too.

"So open the window in your chest.
Let the invisible fly in and out."

Lesson #3

"*The invisible is more existent than all the visible things.*
Talmud says.
Still, when you leave your body there's not much to stand on.
And there's a crack in the cosmic egg.
Truth is, this world is just one side of the nothing
that's on the other side."

Lesson #4

"Now I'll tell you about death.
Life has an eye to see, says Talmud,
              but what do you think Death has?
Death is made of eyes,
            made of eyes, dressed in eyes.
And when she comes, she comes with a knife
    in her hands.
And you go through the wall and it's a flaming word.

Death is what happens when all you have left
    is the life that was there all along.
But remember: you're still gonna need money
    when you die."

FATHER, ONE WEEK DEAD, STROLLING UP PALM CANYON BOULEVARD

Palm Springs, CA

He wears a green surgical gown,
bristly white moustache and
a cheery, contented smile.

Shoe- and sock-shaped clouds above,
ghost-dog on a leash
gliding beside him.

"Smell that?" he says, lighting a Camel,
"that's it, son,
                    the aroma of the afterlife.

"Put someone in the ground
and you think he's gonna stop?
You're thinking the dead
                    shouldn't enjoy themselves?

"Anyway, my being dead counts for something;
listen to me, son. There's a saying:
You don't really belong to a place
until you bury your father there."

"Welcome to California!" says Leopard Dog.
"His death is your ticket. Tell me,
what were you before?
A floater, that's what you were."

"And there's a reason," Father says:
"a man needs a connection, someone on the inside.
As above, so below.
You've got an in in both worlds."

"That's right. And a dog, too,"
says Dog.

DOG DOOR TO HEAVEN

>"*As spirit guide, whose job it was to guide his master into the next life and then to testify as to his master's goodness, dogs of intense devotion and loyalty were needed... As pets they have been affectionately raised as loyal companions... [and] as tools in the treatment of rheumatism.*"
>—Ery Camara, "Looking at the Xolo," artnet.com

Dog:
"I can out-think, out-work, out-fight any dog
      in that world or in this.
Woof fuckin' woof. I told you before, I'm here
to look after your father. Relax, dammit!
Besides, like the man said, 'Death is an illusion.'
B̲ow wow, b̲ow wow!
Anyway, who else is gonna lie against him,
      draw rheumatism from his body?
    Leopard dog, that's who.
Even now he sleeps with his hands on me—
    osteo-arthritis—
that need healing. Yeah, even in heaven.
Truth is, dogs are doctors, too.
    Heaven, this 'other side,'
is one big hospital and, like I told you,
    it's filled with dogs,
New Guinea Singing dogs, Xolos, Leopard dogs, dogs
    that listen to you and protect you.
You think someone dies and God's gonna make them
    whole again?
God's not perfect either. W̲oof, woof!
People say 'Heaven is a place that cannot be found,'
but if you got a dog,
    you can find it."

DOG, WITH FATHER, AT THEIR EASE IN HEAVEN

"Bow wow, BOW wow. You know what heaven is?
Dogs, dogs and people,
      dogs, everywhere, dogs—and people
who can't be without them.

"Listen to me. You put a dog in this place
and you think he's gonna stop being a dog?
Or people? The dead don't change.
Whatever they were in life, they are now.
Look at your father over there, smoking;
you think because a person's dead, he's done?
Done? Done what?

"And God? Sonny, He's not going to help you.

"Anyway, everything oscillates
between is and is not.
On, off. On, off.
Yes, no. Yes, no.
Aristotle said it.
      There's howling
           and there's howling necessity.
     There's the way things are
and the way they really are.

"So, the dead don't want to hear you carrying on.
      Mourn,
if you want to, but mourn with your mouth shut.
The dead don't want to hear it.
Forgive the dead for their mortality.
Forgive your father, Sonny, forgive him
for being dead."

A MAN NEEDS A PLACE TO STAND

"Snap out of it, son!
    Yes, of course I'm dead,
but you think I've left the world?
Then how come you're talking to me?
Nu? ask yourself:
    How is this possible? Listen to me:
There's more good news.
That's right: Death doesn't separate you from God.
    This is a surprise? You were thinking
        there's something to fear?
Anyway, wait till you die, son. You'll see.
We never entirely leave the world.
Ach, there's no 'there' to leave. There's hardly a 'here.'
And you, *nudnik*,
    you just think you have a body.
Still, you can't chase the invisible.
Do that and you'll end up everywhere,
    and then what?
A man needs a place to stand."

LIFE IS ITS OWN AFTERLIFE

"Enough already. Mourn,
        mourn all you want…
What good will it do?
Truth is, I feel great, son. Never better!

"So what if I'm invisible?
So what if I'm dead?
You don't need a body to be a *mensch*,
        a man of substance.
Ach, but with a body at least
you've got some privacy.
Without a body you can't conceal anything.

"There's more, son,
        and bad news for you.
This will surprise you—
when you die one of the first questions God asks is,
        'Did you marry?'
Turns out after God created the world, the rest of the time
He spent making marriages.
So a couple, when they meet, it's *bashert*,
        'it was meant to be.'
That's so… that's how
        together they fulfill their destiny.
But divorce, that they don't allow.
So you won't be coming.

        But thank God
    for what you've got.
What are you missing? Not much. There is no afterlife,
        not really.
That's right, son.
Life is its own afterlife."

FROM BEYOND THE GRAVE, THE PODIATRIST COUNSELS HIS SON ON PRAYER

"How to pray?
You're gonna need a password.
But not now. And you're gonna see
it's numbers, not words. Didn't I tell you: if it's got words,
it's not prayer, and it's not a password either.
So what if I'm dead? What does that matter?
You think you bury your father and that's the end?
Schmegegge! What are you thinking, that the living
    have a monopoly on life?
Give the dead some credit.
I didn't just die, you know. Think of the preparation. A man
has to get himself ready. And what did I ask?
That you pay your respects. So light the *yizkor*,
    light the candle. *Oi*!
Tear the clothes, rend the garment, I said, and that you did.
Point my feet toward the door, I said, and that you did.
God takes what He takes, son, and the body follows.
But prayer? Prayer? Where was the prayer?
Listen: God created us first the feet,
    then the rest.
So? So we bow the head when we pray
to show respect. Cover the head,
where's your *yarmulke*? *Daven, daven*,
rock back and forth… Now ask:
'Who am I? Who *am* I?
What am I here for?'

These are the things you ask,
> but this is not prayer.

It's what you need to know before you start.
Why are we here? We're here to mend the world.
> That's it.

Just remember, God doesn't answer prayers.
So don't ask.
Don't ask for anything.
Shopping is shopping. Prayer is prayer.
Don't confuse the two."

THIS IS A FATHER

"Where are you going?
That you don't know, do you?
Yes, it's me. Who else would it be?
You think I don't see what you're up to?
Wait, I'm not finished.
He's in such a hurry to leave
    but he doesn't know the address.
Walk, walk, that he knows, the easy part.
How will you end up?
You think I'm hard on you? I'm not hard enough.
Where do they come from,
    smart guys like you?
And where do they go?
Head at one end, feet at another.
What kind of creature is this?
Meshuggener, a crazy man.
Two billion times in a lifetime it beats,
    the heart.
And the brain, three and a quarter pounds,
200 billion neurons. And for what?
To walk. What, again!
Walks out on a wife.
Walks out on a child.
You I didn't walk out on.
For you I stayed—even now,
I may be dead, that's true,
but I'm not going anywhere.
This is a father."

NOTES

Science of the Unseen
"The wise man sees in Self those that are alive and those that are dead." In his Introduction to *Patanjali's Aphorisms of Yoga*, translated by Shree Purohit Swami, W.B. Yeats quotes this line from the *Chandogya-Upanishad*.

"Spirit alone has value, Spirit has no value. Eternity expresses itself through contradictions."—W.B. Yeats.

Yeats' book, *The Rose*, draws heavily on Rosicrucian symbolism. As a child, I had no inkling that the "Yeats" my father quoted was a poet. Up until the time I started college, Yeats, for me, was this Rosicrucian who wrote commentaries on texts my father brought into our previously Jewish home.

Rosy Cross Father. "We are the bees of the golden hive of the invisible." The phrase originates in a letter by Rainer Maria Rilke concerning his *Duino Elegies*.

Rilke writes ". . . It is our task to imprint this temporary, perishable earth into ourselves so deeply, so painfully and passionately, that its essence can rise again, 'invisibly,' inside us. We are the bees of the invisible. We wildly collect the honey of the visible, to store it in the great golden hive of the invisible. *The Elegies* show us at this work, the work of the continual conversion of the beloved visible and tangible world into the invisible vibrations and agitation of our own nature."

Lenore and the Leopard Dog. "There is man and woman and a third thing, too, in us," says the poet. Here I must credit the amazing Jelaluddin Rumi.

I am indebted to Paul Foster Case for his book, *The True and Invisible Rosicrucian Order*, which provides an analysis of both the pre- and post-Mason Rosicrucians..." Case has defined Rosicrucianism as "Christian Hermeticism allied with Kabbalah." Dad's journey from Orthodox Judaism to Rosicrucianism was not so great a stretch as I first imagined.

Rosicrucian. AMORC, Ancient Mystical Order Rosae Crucis.

A search on the Internet brings up scores of references, past and present, to "Kit Kat," including a) the four-finger Kit Kat chocolate crisp and b) Kit Kat clubs in Berlin, London, Chicago and San Jose, CA (motto: "have a drink and enjoy the view"). In my experience, Kit Kat Clubs are typically wide for "close up" seating and have low ceilings for the illusion of intimacy.

I am using "Kit Kat Club" in this volume in a generic way. Any resemblance to Kit Kat Clubs, or to former employees and performers, living or dead, is purely coincidental.

* * *

KIT KAT CLUB, HISTORY (1711—)

"...That enterprising bookseller [Jacob Tonson] had founded a club called the Kit Kat Club which met at the eating-house of a certain Christopher Catt, famed for his mutton pies. The club had thirty-nine members, almost all leading members of the Whig party, and to it Addison was introduced by its founder.

"The Kit Kat buzzed with news in these days. Marlborough was at the height of his military fame, and when London heard of the victory of Blenheim, on the 2nd of August, 1704, the club felt that a triumph so great must be celebrated in verse. Halifax recommended Addison for the task, and the Chancellor of the Exchequer, visiting him in his humble lodgings over a shop, commissioned him to write a poem..."
—From *The Age of Addison*, by Anna M. Pagan

* * *

THE PLAY "CABARET"

The play "Cabaret" is set in the Kit Kat Club in 1929-1930 Berlin. It is there that the star, Sally Bowles, entertains with song and dance performers, the Kit Kat Girls and Kit Kat Boys. The music of Kander & Ebb is played by the Kit Klub Band and includes such hits as *Willkommen, Cabaret, Mein Herr, What Would You Do* and *Maybe This Time*.

* * *

Photo: Lynn Lundstrum Swanger

LOUISIANA CATAHOULA LEOPARD DOG —RARE BREED

Description: Short coat colored in a bluish gray or black/tan pattern. Weight up to 80 pounds, with deep chest, good heart and superior lung capacity. Legs solid and strong boned.
Temperament: Very intelligent, independent, territorial. Not for the casual pet owner. A protective, yet dominating canine.
Origin: Louisiana is believed to have been the point of origin and the breed has been designated the state dog of Louisiana.